Echoes in the Wind

Another book by Richard I. Thorman
From Cynwyd Castle on Jackson's Point
Poetry and Prose
ISBN 0-9680045-6-3

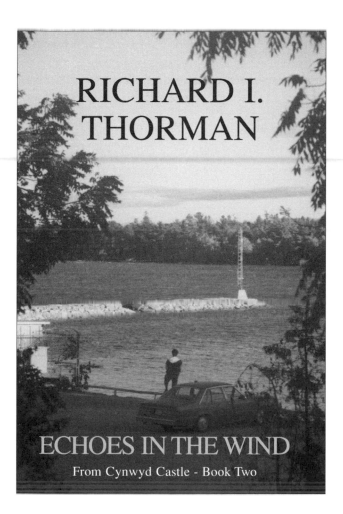

RICHARD I. THORMAN

ECHOES IN THE WIND

From Cynwyd Castle - Book Two

Canadian Cataloguing in Publication Data.

Thorman, Richard I. (Richard Iorweth), 1929-
    Echoes in the wind

Poems.
ISBN 0-9689017-0-0

    1. Title

PS8589.H5494E34 2001   C811'.54   C2001-901212-8
PR9199.3.T46E34 2001

Photographs by Richard I. Thorman.

Published by Cynwyd Castle Books,
278 Bloor Street East - #1802,
Toronto, Ontario.
M4W 3M4

    Printed in Canada by Coach House Printing Company.

For my beloved family
and friends,
including Bernice Lever,
whose editorial assistance
is gratefully acknowledged.

CONTENTS

three - history

four - habituation

five - hardiness

PREFACE

My interest in tradional and structural poetry of earlier ages surfaces in selected poetic formats including villanelle, triolet, tanka and haiku. I have tried to achieve a reasonable balance between form and content in the pursuit of themes. However, I should warn you that I have been unable to suppress my wry sense of humour which bubbles to the surface now and then.

Book two in the Cynwyd Castle series continues under the influence of the creative venue which the castle provided. Two items of note are the brief history of the property and Ill Winds, a fictional story of survival in a frigid hell of gale winds, blinding snow, broken ice and open water on Lake Simcoe.

The Lester B. Pearson Garden was sent to the participants in its dedication. The honourable Herb Gray, Deputy Prime Minister of Canada responded - "Your poem captures the beauty and the tranquillity of the Garden and I appreciate you sharing it with me."

I was deeply moved by the ceremonies surrounding the return of an unknown soldier from World War I for interment in the National War Memorial in Ottawa in May of 2000. Certain of the poems convey my thoughts on this and similar reminders of the darker side of the human psyche.

The award-winning Morning Serenity has been reprinted to draw attention to the fact that it has been deposited in the City of Scarborough Bicentennial Time Capsule to be opened in January 2046, and you are all invited to attend.

Richard Iorweth Thorman,
May, 2001.

ONE

HEARTLAND

WHITE WATER

In calm of mid day
the inlet soundly sleeps
in warmth of sun.

Roaring, the seaplane takes off
dragging white water behind.

MORNING SERENITY

Looking out over the frozen lake
this lazy morning of early spring,
thoughts float aimlessly
on some distant Sargasso sea.

Monotonous line of distant shrouded mystery
teases memory of twinkling night shores
and winking shoal markers.

Eye-squinting reflected light blurs mind images
as a Great Grey Owl unusually far from home
perches on a dark branch sculpture listening
for non resident bog lemmings and red-backed voles.

Wind traces and skidoo rubbings
in filigreed oriental designs of spectrum whites
grace the crystal comforter of sleeping waters.

> I and the spirit lake
> are as one
> in the quiet being
> of the moment.

Grand Award Winner in the Scarborough Arts Council 1996 Poetry
Contest and deposited in the City of Scarborough Bicentennial Time
Capsule to be opened in January 2046.

CHILDREN ON BEACHES

1. strolling in bare feet
    baked by tropical white sands . . .
    snow storms seem mere words

2. laughing children guide
    silver mylar hoops on high
    as shells hum shanties

3. small hands in motion
    sculpt dream castles in warm sand . . .
    Live long new boy king!

4. castles in the sand . . .
    ageing ramparts and dry moats
    strangely deserted

5. Alberta Clippers
    bring frosty arctic air south . . .
    bikinis shiver

TOMORROWS' DAY

Frolicsome sunbeams
awaken primary colours
on aged glass
as organ compositions
blend memories
and solemnity
in family and friends.

A trio in white
and diapers
listens and watches
not understanding
the coming together
of diverse beginnings.

vows
of love
and
commitment
echo
in line
with
those
before.

Eroding red clay brick
of the church exterior
is a reminder of
humanity's frailty
as it reaches to touch
unknown tomorrows.

NAME DAY

How shall we sign you
Now on a canvas of life
Sweet innocent child

Elders meet for the naming
Soft rain, turbulent thunder

This is a Tanka in which the first three lines were written by Richard I. Thorman and the responding two lines by Evelyn Catharine Yates.

YOUNG IN LOVE

When they were young in love they fell

Love others thought would never end

But some things they could not foretell

When they were young in love they fell

Life can become a living hell

Which only parting can transcend

When they were young in love they fell

Love others thought would never end

OUR MAJOR

It is said that money can't buy happiness,
but purchase a puppy and share your home
with it for sixteen years and you find out
that the old adage isn't always true.

For the children, Major was as much a member
of the family as any of the adults and a reliable
companion when grown ups weren't available
to romp and frolic and hug and kiss and comfort.

At the animal hospital I couldn't talk because
my throat was so choked up. I signed your death
warrant with a heavy heart even knowing that
I had no choice and that you would understand.

You were a loyal, faithful and loving friend for so long.
It won't be easy to adjust to your absence, but I have
a feeling that wherever dogs go when they die, you will
still remember us. Certainly, we won't forget you.

CHRISTMAS EVE

As night descends round the earth
      and the light show of the heavens
            signals Christmas Eve,

thoughts of children and some adults
      transcend barriers of language,
            religion, race and wealth,

enjoined in a fervent wish
      that all humankind may find
            peace and freedom from fear.

TRILOGIA OF BEING

(All religions are paths up a mountain in the direction of the source of cosmic truth)

1. From the crucible of the universe, they come,
   Components of matter and energy to be molded
   By a formula known only to an intelligence
   Capable of creations beyond the comprehension
   Of mortal beings which issue fearlessly
   From the womb of women into the unknown of life.

2. From the moment a newborn's senses register
   To the reality of his or her environment
   And eyes open to behold the predestined beginning
   Of existence, all is pleasure and pain.
   In the amalgam of random purpose and chance,
   All is a product of chaotic uniqueness.

3. As the beginning is a step into the unknown, so is death
   And although the time preceding the moment of change
   May be anywhere in the spectrum from utter confusion
   To quiet waiting, the transition for all is a step into
peace
   As borrowed elements are returned and the energy
   Of past existence is enjoined again with the eternal.

LAST GOODBYE

"This is the T.D. Acres Nursing Home. Your sister Ruth is failing, and we don't know how long she has. Maybe you should come over soon."

Not unexpected, but still a shock. My heart sinks in spite of the agonizing hours of the past ten years as I lived with the gradual stripping of her identity by Alzheimer's disease and tried to prepare myself for the inevitable end.

You take for granted the closeness when young. The times she messed around with mother's makeup and other mischief, and with big brown eyes could swear innocence and be convincing. I miss those big brown eyes the most. Tears could come at will and disappear just as quickly. She would always fall for my practical jokes and tricks, but I would never hurt her feelings. I know she loved me.

On her death bed, her breaths exited her open mouth in forced puffs. Her lips were dry. Eyelids partially covered the eyes but at different levels. It was her, but it wasn't. She had died months before when she no longer recognized me. I bent over and kissed her forehead and said softly, "I love you, dear Ruth. Goodbye."

Oblivious to family gathered for the death watch, I straightened up, and with throat constricted by emotion, had to walk out of the room. I circled the hallways of the floor seeing others still hanging on to something which Ruth was about to let go.

Somewhat under control, I returned to the room and said goodbye to her two sons. The body which breathed life for another four hours did not require my bedside presence.

It was six months before I could look at her picture on the TV console. Now, I can.

A SIX YEAR OLD'S PERSPECTIVE

"Mary Edna Thorman (McMillan) of Toronto and Jackson's
Point passed away in her 89th year on Wednesday, March
18th 1998 after a short illness." - Toronto Star.

And the mother explained to her children,
"God chose Aunt Eddie to be an angel
And she will be very happy in heaven
Because she will be with her sister again,
Looking down and watching over us."

And the young daughter said,
"Her sister will have brought
Aunt Eddie's angel wings down to her
And they will have flown
Back to heaven together."

NOCTURNES

As the lingering iridescence of a summer sunset fades into the dark hues of a night sky, I close my eyes and allow my physical being to settle slowly into the time-shaped contours of the upholstered arm-chair rocker. Within my enveloping reverie, residual images left by the departed sun are joined by the pensive refrain of Chopin's Nocturne Opus 55, No. 1. In the silence of the darkening Great Hall of Cynwyd Castle on Jackson's Point, phantom felt hammers gently vibrate spectral piano strings in the colours of the night.

From some early nineteenth century Parisian habitation, a young man, who would never reach forty years of age, penned the quiet reflective composition whose notes now play andante in my head. This uncomplicated nocturne from the romantic period of music has joined the everflowing stream of exceptional musical expression from the past. That the quiet pensive mood of the composer can be communicated over the years, as with voices of long dead poets, is an endowment beyond comprehension.

When the sounds of this cerebral concert diminish into silence, my eyes open to the darkened cavern of the Great Hall and focus on the windows in the north wall which tonight feature an extravaganza of sparkling stars in astronomical roles with prancing moonbeams on lake waters, accompanied by the symphonic sounds of wind spirits and night creatures in another nocturne.

CYNWYD CASTLE

Cynwyd Castle is located on land jutting into Lake Simcoe known as Jackson's Point. On the south it looks out over the marina harbour, and on the north over the broad expanse of the lake. The building sits on a high cliff top with lawns which gradually slope eastward to the water and an underwater lot of some two hundred feet in length. At sundown, the tower of St. George's Church is visible across the bay on Sibball's Point. The church cemetery is the resting place of Stephen Butler Leacock and Mazo de la Roche, two well known Canadian authors, and Captain William Bourchier.

The history of the property officially begins in 1818 when Captain Bourchier of the Royal Navy was granted twelve hundred acres in recognition of his service in the war of 1812. The parcel included the present townsites of Sutton and Jackson's Point. On April 18th, 1821, Captain Bourchier married Amelia Jackson. She was a daughter of John Mills Jackson who in 1828 purchased the land then known as Frying-Pan Point, and built a comfortable log cabin thereon. In time, it became know as Jackson's Point.

In 1867, John McDonald et al purchased the property and in 1871, Levi Miller received title to the underwater lot. Both men were partners in the Lake Simcoe Transportation and Dry Dock Company which operated the marine railway and dry dock at Jackson's Point and the Enterprise, a twin screw steamer which plied Lake Simcoe and Couchiching from 1883 to 1903. The Enterprise is said to be the inspiration for Stephen Leacock's Mariposa Belle in Sunshine Sketches of a Little Town.

In 1927, Irving E. Robertson purchased the land and began to construct the building know as Cynwyd Castle. The same year, he was married in the Presbyterian Church on

Dalton Road in Sutton. His was the first marriage performed in the newly completed church. Irving Robertson was the owner of The Toronto Evening Telegram which had been founded in 1876 by John Ross Robertson.

The property remained in the hands of the family until 1952 when it was sold to Shouldice Hospital Ltd. which held the property until 1973.

Richard I. Thorman purchased the property on March 8th, 1993. A two year restoration was commenced with the aim of recreating the elegance and charm of a residence designed for a wealthy family of the early thirties.

The project included: repairing a leaking roof which had damaged ceilings, walls and floors; repointing of exterior masonry which had left the stone cladding in danger of collapse; replacing windows and doors; upgrading of electrical service, heating and insulation; major work in the Florida room; clearing the grounds of scrub growth to provide an eastern vista of lake and sunrise; stablizing the shoreline by importing ice-age boulders and creating an ecologically-friendly buffer against the eroding power of waves and ice.

When the job was completed, it was named Cynwyd Castle after a small village of ancient times located high in the hills of North Wales where relatives of Mr Thorman still reside. A plaque on the front of the home was commissioned and crafted in England; it included the red dragon of Welsh heraldry. .

The interior of the Castle is rich in panelling and wide-planked floors. The "Great Hall" is twenty-four feet by thirty-four feet and along with the formal dining room serves as the focal point for family gatherings and the entertainment of guests. The staircase in the main entrance hall leads up to the family room with its picture window providing spectacular views of Lake Simcoe and its all-season activities. There are five panelled bedrooms and a cosy den with fireplace in the "Tower". A service door opens from the den into the self-contained "Servants Quarters" over the garage with its private entrances to street and waterfront. In addition, there are four bathrooms, two fireplaces, a large kitchen, pantry and Florida room.

Richard Iorweth Thorman, BCom, CA was Comptroller of Finance of The Metropolitan Toronto School Board during the period of explosive growth in enrolment from 1958 to 1980, the Vice President and Comptroller of the Canadian operations of the Prudential Insurance Company of America from 1981 to 1986, a developer of Vanvalley Estates in Whitchurch-Stouffville, and a farmer in the Queensville area. His credits as author and poet include works in the United States Library of Congress and Onteris, and in over 30 collections and anthologies. In 1997, his book, From Cynwyd Castle on Jackson's Point, was released.

The property was sold on December 7th, 1999. Its future will unfold as the fates decree. Esto Perpetua.

TWO

HABITAT

MOUNTAIN LOG HOME

In the high woods it stands,
ageing cabin of dreams.

Did Saturday bring friends
from over nearby hills?
Did fiddle and banjo
set toes and hearts thumping
to old time country tunes?

Did odours of fresh bread
and hearty oven fare
permeate the kitchen
drawing children and adults
to its warmth in winter?

Did romance blossom here
in the leafy bowers
of maple and pine stands
and did the union bring
new life to spread the seed?

Memories from the past
benignly haunt old homes.

SUMMER RAIN

Under a windless sky of iron grey,
The falling rain transforms the lake
Into a paisley domain of faded blues.

The gentle shower causes drops
On maple leaves to gather and elongate
Before plunging to jostle those below.

Trees whisper to caressing touches
As multicoloured petunias bow down
To release nectar-flavoured ambrosia.

A squirrel pauses high on a dead branch
To groom its rain-soaked fur
And to flick moisture from a soggy tail.

Spiders huddle in the dryness of cracks
Abandoning their sagging tapestries
To entrapped gems and silver mists.

Images in reflecting pools on asphalt
Distort as each raindrop creates
Overlapping circles and tiny waves.

The air smells fresh and earthy
With mixed scents of undergrowth
Turning emerald green in the dull light.

I have an urge to fling off my clothes
And join the frolic of the Little Folk
Who surely are about in the dance.

NORTHERN PARKLANDS

Ribbons of asphalt
drape pragmatic ugliness
on virgin landscape
like raw obscene graffiti
on grey public walls.

Noise of man's engines
shatter pristine sound
of wilderness sanctuary
like out-of-tune string sections
in symphony's Strauss waltz.

Campers and out trips
intrude on wildlife domain
altering natural habitat
like pushers in neighbourhoods
destroying minds and futures.

Exhaust fumes and smoke
drift through evergreen forests
masking fragile scents
like cheap cologne and perfume
pollute air around humans.

Lofty noble creeds
cite unspoiled northern parkland
preserved for future;
like New Year's resolutions -
great to make, easy to break.

THE ORIENTAL FAN

Delicate fingers
Gently hold the fragile fan
Gossamer moment

The opening fan
Reveals magic of the brush
Poppies spring to life

White paint masks the souls
Fans blend with body motions
Geishas entertain

Rhythms of the fan
Ripples in the universe
Reaching for the stars

RHYTHMS

1. Pulse beats resonate softly
   through the downy fill of pillow
   as mind gradually sets adrift
   stressful challenges of the day.

2. By the window in a nursing home
   a fragile figure contemplates
   the blurred shapes of the seasons
   as they cycle in predictable order.

3. Ancestors shuffle bare feet,
   clap hands and vocalize
   in respect and celebration of
   powerful spirits sustaining life.

4. A thin gold line marches in quartz
   cadence round the face of time
   while planets move to a composition
   choreographed for a celestial cosmos.

NATURE'S UNIVERSE

Walk
a narrow footpath
above the tree line
in Canadian Rockies
far from census tracts
and be aware
one is not alone
in such works of creation.

Note
what the eyes behold
with new innocence,
sky-high mountain peaks,
hazy, verdant valleys,
and be humbled
by living cycloramas
mid the majesty of scale.

See
bluebells at your feet
their blossoms swaying
in fragrant, gentle breezes
of rugged wilderness
and be as one
in spirit and soul
within nature's universe.

MAYTIDE

In Maytide
    one can rove among
fresh blossoms
    hearing love songs sung.

Though seasons
    change and time flows on
Yet flowers
    bloom in Avalon.

TOTEM

The eagle feather,
an aboriginal totem,
is set before me.
I hesitate to speak.

The feather
in aura of mystery
casts its spell.
I stroke its quill.

I sense the presence
of humanity's source;
my spirit-self awakens.
I am once more.

In peace, I set aside
the past and future
to release the moment.
I begin to speak.

THREE

HISTORY

Part I - WEAVINGS

Dancing fingers
   relive traditions
as yarn-dyed strands
    emerge in heavy
      reversible illusions;

Like tapestries,
   lives emerge as
amalgams of life-dyed strands
    from those they meet and
      those who came before.

Part II - SHADOWS IN WEAVINGS

Dancing fingers,
   conjuring shadows from Mongolian merry-making,
relive traditions
   handed down in umber-smoked interiors of hide-covered
   tents,
as yarn-dyed strands
  . . . emerge in heavy reversible illusions;

Like tapestries,
   awaiting return to dust in soundless mystery,
lives emerge as,
   awash in blood, pain, love, and alone,
amalgams of life-dyed strands
  . . . from those they meet and those who came before.

LESTER B. PEARSON GARDEN

The opening ceremony and dedication of The Lester B. Pearson Garden for Peace and Understanding at Victoria University in the University of Toronto was held on October 14th, 2000.

The Man

"Educated persons ... will place the desire to put muscle into missiles ... below the desire to put dignity and decency into living; moral values into action; beauty into words and images. They will put the search for the good life in peace and freedom above every other search ..." — Lester B. Pearson.

The Pond

Share a moment of silence with a glistening black crow
as from atop the balustrade it decides if the pond
and its environs are of any interest.

Cast a grain of sand in a tranquil corner of reflecting
waters
and perhaps discover enlightenment
in the significance of imperceptible ripples.

Pause quietly by pond's edge
if you would hear a cradle lullaby of falling waters
from the symphony of first life.

Imagine creations of Earth Mother in lifeless foliage
sparkle white from North Winds airbrushing moist vapours
in advance of the resurrection of Spring.

The Garden

Clusters, leaves, bungleweed, plumes, petals, cones,
ground cover, flowers, spikes, stems, bushes, trees, bells.

	Flowers
blue	*Ajuga*
red	*Anemone*
green, pink	*Astilbe, Bergenia*
magenta rose	*Rose Campion*
purple, orange, etc.	*Echinacea, Geranium*
ginger	*Asarum (Wild Ginger)*
blue, deep shades	*Globe Thistle, Heuchera*
purple, silver, yellow	*Hosta, Lamium, Ligularia*
earthy, black-eyed Susan	*Pachysandra, Rudbeckia*
grey-green, white	*Russian Sage, Sweet Woodruff*
creamy	*Solomon's Seal*
	Trees & Shrubs
dark green to reddish purple	*Kousa Dogwood*
Fall colours	*Siebold Maple, Japanese Maple*
dark reddish purple	*Japanese Stewartia*
rosy purple	*Shrub Bushclover*

Graceful, drooping, wild, exotic, textured, deep, whorled,
arching, intense, pyramidial, Winter, Spring, Summer, Fall.

The Visitor

A leaf enters
the autumn ballet
to unpredictable
curtain calls
from spirit airs
  while

windstrong airfoil
descends on course
to rearrange
the unstillable
mirrored firmament.

Black-eyed
Susan dwarf
in paling pastels
stolidly faces
its soon-to-be
    while
jackhammers and diesels
in dissonant cadence
challenge
the burbling enthusiasm
of cascading waters.

Slapshots in yellow plastic
carry forward laughter
from less intense times
to whet the appetite
of inquisitive minds
    while
in grip of stone
"The Truth Shall Make You Free"
although to hold a handful of sand
is to wonder if any struggle
could be more elusive.

THE ETERNAL ENIGMA OF ROME

Oh, descendants of the twin sucklers of the bitch wolf, I have seen your works, awesome relics of an empire which stretched throughout the Mediterranean and beyond. Ruins in stone and masonry, which have stood against earthquake and plundering builders of later eras, speak loudly of your legacy of law and state power.

Oh, adherents of Peter, I have walked your spacious square and entered the cool timeless space of your domed cathedral and been overcome by its magnificence and continued influence on spiritual life around the world. In a time when violence and inhumanity seem too prevalent it is reassuring to know that the message of peace still sounds.

Oh, Michelangelo Buonarotti, talented artist from a misty past when your heart beat strong, your mind soared in the raptures of earthly being and your fingers worked marble and tinted plaster, we thank you for the eternal inspiration of the Pieta, the youthful David and the Creation of the Universe in the ceiling frescoes of the Sistine Chapel.

Oh, you seven hills of Latium on the banks of the mighty Tiber, don't ever desert us. In some magical way you cause mankind to pause mid the distractions of everyday life and contemplate the potential in each moment. You have made us understand that the future we dream about can be a reality if only we utilise the powers within us.

LA SAGRADA FAMILIA

In the noonday sun, the unfinished masterpiece
of the architect Antoni Gaudi sits in quiet serenity,
its stone and masonry, a monument in golden tan
mid the hustle of contemporary Barcelona.

Rounded walls of the towers stretch skyward
in gentle slopes to the sunbursts at their apex,
darkened interiors visible through finely detailed
openings adding a seclusive aura to the design.

The church has been under construction since 1882,
rising from its foundations under the direct supervision
of a man synonymous with Spain's Art Nouveau
movement, the modernistas, when he died in 1926.

The dream which inspired this singular architect
can only be speculated upon by those who struggle
to complete the structure because there were never
any architectural drawings or sketches ever found.

With some men and women their aspirations live on
after the brick and mortar have long past into ruin;
with others, the solid remains of past monuments
leave mysterious evidence of dreams long forgotten.

REMNANTS OF THE TITANIC

Memories concealed
By tons of icy water
Holding onto time
Chimes cease in gilded cases
April fifteenth nineteen twelve

Liner Titanic
In black Atlantic Ocean
Over two miles deep
Her final resting place seen
Through underwater filming

Remnants chill the mind
Abandoned doll's face staring
Near bench arabesque
Dinner plate settings washed clean
By discerning hands of fate

Stringed orchestra plays
Tchaikovsky and Puccini
In Ritz restaurant
Sound waves travel unsilenced
Through the timelessness of space

Tons of crumbling steel
Become elements of earth
In rust and decay
Monument to man's ego
May the dead yet rest in peace

THE SURVIVOR

I have strolled with death
down sanitized corridors,
holding cooling warmth.

I have glanced at eyes,
their embers glowing
in the unsleeping quiet.

I have listened to gasping
of courage midst
the chorus of technology.

I have screamed
at unbearable pain
as time hung frozen.

I have stood
in halls of honour
and felt the past.

I have stilled my eyes
as the bugle sounded
and flags fell to earth.

I have walked in night mists
where forever young frolic
in garlands of lights.

I have seen the path
which one day
all must follow.

THE UNKNOWN SOLDIER

Prologue:

Thursday, May 25th, 2000 - at the twin white towers of the Vimy Memorial to Canadians who died in World War One, the day begins with a military handover ceremony for an unknown soldier who was killed on the battlefield at Vimy Ridge in France more than eighty years ago. Later in the day, the same pallbearers and Canadian contingent bring the flag-draped coffin into the centre block of the Parliament Buildings of Canada to lie in state for public viewing until moved to its final resting place.

Sunday, May 28th, 2000 - in the afternoon, the coffin is moved in procession with full military honours from the Parliament Buildings to the base of the National War Memorial for a state funeral and entombment.

A Young Man
in a Centennial project led by a determined Royal
Canadian Legion

A Young Man
to represent the sacrifices of patriots through all time -
past, present and future

A Young Man
in a final mission code-named Operation Memoria

A Young Man
brought home with his brass 'Canada' badges in a maple
coffin

A Young Man
handled gently by Army, Navy, Airforce and RCMP pallbearers

A Young Man
draped in a flag he didn't know on a gun carriage pulled by
four majestic horses

A Young Man
whose tombstone is the National War Memorial in his
nation's capital

A Young Man
The Unknown Soldier, Le Soldat Inconnu

A Young Man
in a grey granite sarcophagus with sculpted bronze helmet
and sword

A Young Man
beneath a handful of soil from near Vimy Ridge and each
Canadian province and territory, and an eagle's feather

A Young Man
who journeyed into foreign lands to protect his country

A Young Man
who proffered the price of peace for those he loved

A Young Man
who climbed from a sodden trench to face certain death

A Young Man
who felt the impact of screaming ordnance

A Young Man
whose life ended before it had barely begun

A Young Man
whose hopes and dreams were instantly denied

A Young Man
who died alone in the company of others in a man-made
hell

A Young Man
who was someone's son and 'Missing In Action'

A Young Man
owed a national debt which can never be repaid

A Young Man
among the forever young in too many memories

A Young Man
in the growing ranks of those who pay the price of wars

A Young Man
whose silenced voice may speak loudest against those who
would destroy his country

A Young Man
we will never know but should never forget

WINDS OF CHAOS

*(India conducted nuclear tests on May 11, 1998 and on
May 30th Pakistan did the same.)*

National pride savages
Ideals of humanitarianism
And peaceful coexistence.

Parliamentary trumpets blare,
Like strident harbingers of
death by fireball misadventure.

Snare drums of chaos
Drive cadences of war
Through shadows of despair.

Intellectual contamination
Repeats lessons unlearned
In past confrontations.

KOSOVO

The antiquated diesel tractor and wooden wagon were all that was left of the farm. The driver who stared sombrely ahead was a twelve year old boy with tear-stained cheeks, dust-covered clothes and a cap pulled low over his forehead. The boy's hands gripped the scarred wheel with white-knuckle determination not to stop until the remnants of his family were safely in Albania. Only the sounds of the creaking wagon could be heard as it bounced and jolted along the gravel road. Behind him, with some hastily loaded personal items from their home, were his mother, younger sisters, baby brother and grandmother.

Occasionally an arthritic and age-patterned hand emerged from under black clothes to cover the mouth of the family matriarch as she coughed and with stained white handkerchief, dabbed at watery eyes. Her thoughts were at a temporal distance: 'Fadil, you were a fine man and handsome. I was so proud of you at our wedding. I can still feel your manly touch when you gently pushed the ring on my trembling finger. I miss you my love, but I am glad you are not here to see all this. I know you are at peace and some day soon I will be with you again. For the moment, I must be strong. Fatine and the little ones must survive. I pray our sons are all right, but I have heard stories. However, they are like you, my love, and will fight to live. God willing, they will escape the butchers and I will see them again. We are only a few kilometres from the border, but I worry about the children, for there is only water and food for another meal.'

When the staccato sounds of automatic weapons erupted from the brush-covered hillside overlooking the irregular column, screaming and panicking Kosovars threw themselves into the ditch.

Ali instinctively shifted the tractor into neutral, put the brake on, jumped down and raced to his mother and siblings to help them off the trailer and underneath.. He sped to the far side to help his grandmother, but she was slumped to the side with her blood slowly pooling on the weathered planks of the wagon floor.

CHECHNYA

In deep snows of winter, all hope for Spring.
Yet teenage conscripts continue dying.
Young hearts should fall in love, hear song birds sing.

Rejoice, let loose your pure white doves to wing.
Never weapons of war and death unsling.
In deep snows of winter all hope for Spring.

Exchange grenades for marriage vows and ring.
For everyone's children, peace forever bring.
Young hearts should fall in love, hear song birds sing.

In cold damp bedrolls, their memories cling
In the morn, they must set demons on wing.
In deep snows of winter, all hope for Spring.

No true satisfaction does spilt blood bring.
Power politics are not worth a thing.
Young hearts should fall in love, hear song birds sing.

Let breasts fill with joy, let town square bells ding.
Let's all join hands in a circle and swing.
In deep snows of winter, all hope for Spring.
Young hearts should fall in love, hear song birds sing.

YOUNG CITIZENS

Orphaned innocent
Picks through foul city dump for food,
Haunting big dark eyes
Reflecting images of war.

Anglo-Saxon child,
Shares battered crib with cockroaches,
Living with pee rash, stale smoke,
Loud music and neglect.

Savannah boy cries,
Desert dust caked on teary cheeks,
Hungry flies swarming
Round all moist body openings.

Young citizens,
Some day, the choices will be yours.

SANDBOX OF THE GODS

Amalgams of matter
Splatter the canvas of space
Following predestined routes.

Ancient volcanic rims
Send rock and rubble slides
Rearranging the face of Mars.

Lunar dust devils
Pirouette and leap
Building dunes about the Rover.

On the blue planet
A small brass bell rings
In prepubescent song.

Infinite chaos rules
With order and beauty
In the sandbox of the Gods.

FOUR

HABITUATION

A WRITER'S CONUNDRUM

From the 18th floor
I can look into the sun
and contemplate
existence without shadows,
insulated from the darkness
of a Stygian world

aware reality lurks
in shadowed environs
beyond walls of castle condo
and its comfortable residents,
oblivious to the plight of those
who live on the edge.

THE BAG LADY AND THE STREET KID

I don't know who the street kid was, not even his name. As for the bag lady, her name was Sally, and she died in her sleep of extreme hypothermia one bitterly cold winter night when even her multiple layered attire and the heated exhaust from the sidewalk grates of a downtown office building weren't enough to sustain life. Although her demise took place over two decades ago, she is still very much in my mind, and unknowingly, in the minds of countless others as you will discover when I reveal a secret I have kept buried these many years.

I had just graduated from art school and with the income from a part time job at Eatons had set up bachelor digs cum studio in a rented third floor garret on King Street East west of Parliament Street. As those of you who are familiar with the history of Toronto know, this area has gone steadily down hill from the time the new city hall was constructed at the corner of Bay and Queen Streets in 1890, and the focus shifted from 'Old City', centered at King and Jarvis streets, to 'New City'. Today, the area remains unfocused and is inhabited from a spectrum ranging from neglected and abused street kids to upwardly mobile professionals living in trendy, renovated, red brick Victorian buildings. It has more than its share of crime and violence, but the hazards are not as significant as the artistic inspiration of being close to the heart of the vibrant city.

In those early years when I wasn't working to support myself, I was immersed in art. I never left the studio without my pencils, crayons and sketch book. I loved to sit in the parklike areas surrounding the cathedrals in Old Town and sketch the ones who were attracted to these oases of greenery in the midst of the concrete desert.

As I wandered my special preserve, I began to recognize the regulars as they did me. I suppose I was tolerated and accepted because of my youth and although perhaps deemed odd, nevertheless non threatening. At first, many of the locals would move off if they saw me sketching. Later, they just ignored me. Some would occasionally stroll by and sneak a glance at my efforts, but most would not speak.

One of my favorite subjects was the bag lady known as Sally. You could spot her a mile away. Her shape was unmistakable. In all seasons she wore the castoffs of others in insulating layers which had the effect of expanding her figure to comic matronly proportions. Her straggly dark brown hair streaked with grey puffed out from under her favorite red and white knitted tam. What she wasn't wearing, she carried along with the balance of her belongings in a bundle buggy whose unlubricated axles complained loudly as she moved toward whatever destination was next on the itinerary. Nearly every day, she made the rounds of the cathedral parkettes feeding the squirrels and birds which would excitedly swarm and flutter around her in a display of absolute trust.

At first, my interest was in an overall perspective. Then I began to become aware of those parts of her exposed to view. The hands were deeply tanned and weathered, but not those of a laboring woman. The fingers were long and slender, and with very little imagination, might have belonged to an accomplished violinist or concert pianist. The wrinkled face had a gentle and peaceful quality with no evidence of the anger and lack of hope observable in many street people. The eyes were clear and sparkled when she was amused.

Perhaps fifteen years ago when my reputation as an artist was beginning to take off, I received an unusual telephone call. I was requested to meet with a prospective client in the financial district on Bay Street. When I arrived, I was led by a secretary into an impressive mahogany panelled office and invited to sit in a large overstuffed leather chair. Before I had an opportunity to adequately scan these opulent and unfamiliar surroundings, the door at the side of the room opened, and a silver grey haired man in a navy blue pin stripe entered and sat down behind the desk opposite me.

He took his time before introducing himself and then got right to the point.

"Are you a religious man?" he asked.

I was unprepared for the question and fumbled a reply which I don't recall exactly. I think I told him I attended Sunday School when I was growing up, but now I was not in regular attendance at any church. However, I hastened to add, I did enjoy going to services at Christmas and Easter in any of the cathedrals which border Church Street. Yes, I thought I was a religious man, and I did believe in God.

Whether my answer satisfied him, I couldn't determine. However, he continued.

"I have seen two or three of your paintings, and although I am no expert in the fine arts, they appeal to me. Whether you can manage what I propose is something I want to explore. He paused for another uncomfortable period in which I struggled not to avert my eyes.

"What do you have in mind?"

The executive leaned back in his chair and took a deep breath which he slowly exhaled. "My wife who passed away recently had a sincere interest in theology. Our vacations always included visits to local places of worship, even those not of our faith. She was particularly moved by works of art. I'll never forget when we visited the Vatican. She got quite emotional when she first laid eyes on the Pieta and the ceilings of the Sistine Chapel. I could go on. But let me say simply that my wife was a deeply religious person, and I want to commission an oil painting of some spiritual significance to donate to our church in her memory. Would you be interested?"

I hesitated, trying to sort out my thoughts. I could use the money, but I wasn't too comfortable with the general subject matter. "It's such a broad area. It would be like competing with Michelangelo and other great religious artists. . . . Although I studied most of them in art school and undoubtedly have been influenced to some extent, what I do is a combination of who I am, the skills I have acquired and what I feel when I'm painting. . . . If I accept the commission, I have to be unrestricted in the selection and artistic rendering of the subject matter."

"What happens if I'm not satisfied with the final result?"

"Well, although I would make every effort to please you, there is always the possibility you might end up with a painting you didn't like. To be frank, I haven't had experience with religious themes. My approach would be to select something from the bible, perhaps a parable or event which had visual possibilities. The challenge would be to create an illusion in time and space which communicated the essence of a basically abstract idea."

Our meeting continued for another half hour and ended with both parties coming to an agreement. For better or worse, the commission was mine.

The next few months were hell. The more I tried to come up with something I could work with, the more I became frustrated. Drawing after drawing piled up around the studio. I was on the verge of phoning my client and resigning. But I knew that in spite of my urging him to keep the project a secret, he hadn't. A church official let slip that arrangements were underway for a gala unveiling, etc. etc.

etc. I was in a state of creative block and paralyzing panic.

In the depth of despair, I decided to quit and suffer the consequences. I would phone him in the morning. It was past midnight, and I had stripped for bed when a strange thing happened. On impulse, I went to the storage box containing my oldest sketch books. Maybe I thought they would help me to sleep. Maybe I yearned for the happy uncomplicated good old times. Maybe there was some subconscious motive. Who knows?

With pillow propped under my head and covers pulled up, I commenced to flip the pages. Each drawing loosed a string of memories. The people, the places, the seasons flooded back in vivid detail.

Images of the long departed bag lady recalled my youthful fascination for her. Most of the sketches had been in the environs of the cathedrals on Church Street. It struck me as odd that I always found her on the dedicated grounds of the Houses of God. Could it be some form of predestination? Were the images before me meant to be related to the project? I studied each repeatedly until shortly before dawn when sleep could no longer be postponed.

I awoke at noon and pulled on rumpled jeans and T shirt of the night before, gulped down some hastily prepared food and turned to the blank canvas on the easel. My fingers quickly sketched in the outline of the images in my head.

In seven exhausting days, I stepped back from the easel and set down pallet and brushes. The painting was complete.

The presentation took place three weeks later in the old cathedral hall. The stature of my client in the community and the efforts of a professional promoter had resulted in a gathering beyond expectations. Dignitaries of church and state mingled with parishioners and media representatives in a ferment of conversation and stimulation typical of a wine and cheese function. There was growing excitement as the time approached for formalities to commence.

The attention of the assembly was drawn to the stage when those involved in the proceedings took their places and the master of ceremonies stepped to the lectern and commenced to tap and blow into the microphone. Apparently satisfied with the sound system, he looked up, cleared his throat, and the program was underway.

Following introductions and remarks of the dignitaries, my client stepped forward to stand on the right side of the easel. I did likewise on the left. On his signal, we grasped the corners of the black velvet cloth, and with a synchronized flourish, the painting was unveiled.

A figure dressed in flowing white garments of the desert was seated on a weathered wooden bench in front of a whitewashed mud and wattle wall holding a battered copper cooking pot. Her slender hands were engaged in feeding a covey of small birds which fluttered in harmony about her. Beyond the end of the building and in the near distance, a teenage boy draped in white could be seen hoeing in a garden.

There were no angels or heavenly cherubs to be seen, but the face of the female figure had an angelic expression which could not be denied. The eyes were warm and comforting and twinkled at the antics of the smallest of the feathered creatures of God. She had no halo as the old masters would have painted, but the softly blending colors of the sunlight reflecting off the white colored wall of the hut contained the suggestion of an aura. This same phenomenon was duplicated in the pastel colors surrounding the head of the young man in the garden.

Initially, the unveiling was greeted with silence, but then, like the rustle of a sudden gentle breeze blowing through a stand of maples, applause spread throughout the hall. My eyes were drawn to an elderly lady who had clasped her hands to a small gold cross on a chain around her neck and on whose weathered cheeks could be seen tears of joy and adoration.

My models, the bag lady and the street kid, were now part of a much grander concept than they ever could have imagined, but then . . . they always had been.

CREATIVE SPIRIT

creative spirit
   smothers
      in
     Victorian-like
      absolutes

is erased
   by politics
      of
     intellectual
      cleansing

is nurtured
   in the company
      of
     kindred
      spirits

often blossoms
   from the insight
      of
     a misspent
      youth

CITY SIDEWALKS

Survivors,
neglected
bodies
shuffling
towards
the scrap heap
of long gone youth

minds
tangled
in
alcoholism
dementia
and
disfunctionality

mouthing
obscenities
at a God
held responsible
for
a blurred
existence

life
flickering
within
a
vault
of
darkness.

PATCHWORK JUNGLE

Picked before their time
Buds ready to blossom
Abort their beauty.

      Abused children float
      Seeking love from strangers
      Embracing harpies.

Fledglings soaring free
Fall prey to chicken hawks
Their torn entrails rot.

      Teens going on twelve
      Trade bodies for soiled cash
      Breaking someone's heart.

Street kids with tired eyes
Pissing away their lives
For instant fiefdom.

CRAZY ANNIE

She is called Crazy Annie
    in the streets and alleys
        where she lives

She speaks to herself and often everyone about her
understanding babble of babies and young children
when often rapport with adults seems unnecessary.

She dines in the company of pigeons, squirrels, gulls
and sparrows; hugs trees and park sculptures; plays
with old treasures and waltzes with shadows of dawn.

She revels in the uncertain humors of seasonality,
tasting rain, watching pussy willows, tracing sunsets,
humming to fragrant winds and dancing snowflakes.

She shuffles along through harsh realities of living,
knowing she is not alone with pain and adversity,
playing out a unique role in some greater unknown.

She is Crazy Annie
    but she is someone else
        someone special.

INDIAN SUMMER

With legs crossed and bedroll at his side, the young man slumped against the hard masonry of the corner post anchoring the wrought iron fence separating the tranquillity of the groomed expanse of lawn in front of the Manulife office building from the harsh realities of Bloor Street East.
"Spare any change, mister?"

The bony arm which held out the broken foam cup extended from a black T shirt which hung in folds making the imprinted image unrecognisable. His black jeans with soiled folded cuffs had shifted up to reveal thin hairy legs which disappeared into scuffed and age-darkened work boots.
"Spare any change, ma'am?"

In skin tone and physical characteristics, this mendicant appeared a full-blooded Indian carrying genes of early inhabitants of these lands. Though humbled in the polluted wilderness of core Toronto, my impression was that the embers of hope and pride still glowed within this young brave.
"Spare any change, sir?"

Uncut hair hung in black fullness, framing a nose and chin of sculpted prominence. Eyes were dark with an aura of serenity. The voice was gentle with none of the hard edges so often encountered. Unlike many who work the streets for handouts, he was neither drunk nor high on drugs.
"Spare any change, lady?"

If I were a genie, what wish would he chose? To be rich and live in a nearby luxurious residence or to be transported to some place where waters burbled in pristine purity and the

air smelled sweet and fresh, there to live his life with loving wife, laughing children and caring friends?
"Spare any change, mister?"

I drop a few coins in the cup and walk away depressed.
"Thanks mister. Have a good day."

TWO GUYS IN FOOD COURT

You knew Shellie threw Steve out. Yah, I heard. Did you know she's got the apartment and all their stuff and he's in a furnished room? Really, that's not his style. Yah, but he thinks it's only temporary. I wouldn't bet on it; he's okay sober but he's a loudmouth pig when he's high, and she doesn't like the rough stuff. Yah, that was a pretty bad scene at the party last weekend; he wouldn't leave until she got down on her knees and begged him; he says he doesn't remember. I don't care how drunk you get, you always remember something like that; he's damn lucky her brother kept his cool. Yah, I've seen him in action; I think Shellie did what she did for the sake of his kids upstairs. Yah, (Ha Ha) if they'd woke up and started screaming, it would have been game over for Steve; anyway let's forget Steve, I think that relationship is dead, and he's dreaming if he thinks she'll take him back. I don't agree; lots of couples decide to separate for a while to think things out and then move back together and live happily ever after. That's fairy tale stuff; as soon as Shellie starts socializing with her single friends again, she'll meet another guy and poof, instant relationship. Maybe. You know she hasn't lived alone since she started dating, and she has no problems making friends. Well, it's not all Steve's fault; I'd hate if Annie was a flirt like her. Have you moved back in? No, we agreed to spend some time apart, but we're not like Steve and Shellie. Oh? Absolutely! We still have a relationship; we talk on the phone nearly every night and get together for coffee at Dino's twice a week; best of friends. How do you know she isn't seeing someone else? I know Annie wouldn't cheat on me; I trust her and she trusts me. So when are you going to move back in? Well, we're not in any hurry and we're becoming closer; we can talk about anything and not get upset, and you know we couldn't do that before. Are you getting any sex? Well, just between you and me   not since we agreed to a trial separation. . . . Well, Mike, we've been friends a long time and you know I have to say what I'm thinking; should I go ahead? Can I stop you? . . . I believe no sex, no relationship. Well, George, you're entitled to your opinion, but you're wrong (rising); anyways, I have to get back to work. We still have ten minutes. I know, but I have things to do. Whatever you say.

BACHELOR SHOPPING

Every time I go to the pantry or fridge
For something my stomach and brain crave
And it's not there, I write it on a shopping list
Gripped in the mouth of a frog thing
On top of the microwave.

I hate shopping.

When it becomes a choice between starving,
Eating at the local cafe of gastronomic horrors
Or going to the supermarket,
I force myself to the latter option,
Hoping they're open when I get there.

Shopping is the pits.

Supermarkets are like torture theme parks,
Buggies which go any way but straight ahead,
Frozen food aisles simulating polar winters,
Children and seniors playing chicken with carts
And unreadable bar codes on items not tagged.

Post-shopping is happy hour time.

The latest innovation is computer buying
Based on credit card billing over the Internet.
We are told such pay methods are secure . . .
If teenage hackers can infiltrate Pentagon files
And top-secret, star-wars, control systems,
Chances are their munchies will be on my bill.

I shop with cash.

When it comes to writing about food or eating
I have a back-seat nagger, my digestive system.
Right now, comments are becoming loud and windy,
And will become even more so unless I feed it.
The problem is the lunch menu is not haute cuisine,
Being unsalted crackers, mustard, relish and beer.

I suspect I must go shopping . . . soon.

POOPETRY

I am addicted to writing poetry. It's a form of dementia somewhere between the mental state of the unfortunate wackos who live on the streets and the scary wackos in high places with their toys of mass destruction.

I hate when people ask what I do in retirement. If I tell them, they smile and patronize me as though I wasn't playing with a full deck. If I answer nothing, they nod and the inane chatter crap continues. However, I have decided that the next time I am asked what I do, I will reply - "I write poopetry". When my nosy inquisitor leans forward and says "pardon", I will shake my head and respond, "My dear fellow (madam) you must try to keep up with the times. It is an avant-garde form of literature and all the rage or rave among the intelligensia."

I will then expound on iambic pooptamiters, haipoo, free pooverse, limericpoo, rhyming pooplets - well you get the idea.

I'll tell him or her to keep it secret, and it will spread like a viral poo trot. Soon the Associations of Professional Poets will call themselves leagues of poopets and admit to voting status only those who meet the standards of 'professional' poopetry creators. Associate members will be encouraged to study the excretory standards of the voting poopets as they aspire to first class membership.

The reading public will emerge from in front of their boob tubes to discover alternate entertainment in the written word. Like wildfire, poop lyrics will engulf the music industry from rap poopers to country and western full loaders. There will be Hollypoop and Mediapoop awards for best poopscriptor and score pooper, best male and female impooperator and others.

The economy of the world will soar to greater heights as private enterprise capitalizes on this exciting enlightenment. Equity markets will rise exponentially as speculators compete for positions in related company share issues. All because the existence of poopetry was recognised by the general public. Who knows, some living poopets might even start getting paid on a par with hockey and wrestling stars.

Anyways, I write poetry because I want to. Ain't that something.

PUBLIC WASHROOM GRAFFITI

I find the quality of graffiti in public washrooms today disgustingly low. It used to be that drawings were in soft black lead or blue ink with appropriate shading and cross hatching indicating the artists had some degree of talent. But no more, the quicky efforts scratched with unknown hard objects or those free-handed in cheap felt pens are eyesores and leave too much to the imagination. I think that something which could pass for an oriental shrub, an atomic bomb cloud or a grossly mutated phallic symbol is a shameful waste of prime wall space and the misguided perpetrator should be sent to an art school or monastery for appropriate instruction.

I hesitate to comment on the writing for fear that I will lend it a modicum of acceptability. It is obvious that the current generation of toilet-stall writers need to go back to the early grades of elementary school to learn spelling and to discover the existence of such grammatical wonders as sentences and punctuation. I saw one yesterday - 4 gud sexx - and no comma or dash before the phone number. Isn't that disgraceful . . . particularly when the phone number turns out to be the county morgue. Also, something should be done about the defacing of graffiti. I noticed one over the urinal which read - Irene loves (defaced) - accompanied by a drawing which could have been a heart or a bag of nuts (partially defaced). It had the potential to be a nice Valentine from Irene. Now, no one will know if Irene has a boy or girl friend. As well, some killjoy had scribbled in - Irene loves anyone. By the way, there was only a partial phone number.

Before television, public lavatories had a high educational and entertainment value. I remember such literary classics as:

"Don't bother to stand upon the seat,
The crabs in here can jump forty foot."
  and
"We aim to please,
You aim too, please."

Notice the clarity in meaning, the vivid imagery, the meter and rhyming. These writers had a laudable knowledge of the craft and stood on a par with some well-known poets of today.

What made this era of washroom graffiti so entrancing was the variety of styles and subject matter. For example:

"Dead elms are sexier than some blind dates."

Notice the outdoor connection and the conservationist's view of possible use for the discards of the logging industry.

"Flush twice
It's a long way to the kitchen"

Obviously written by someone sensitive to the problems of the restauranteur.

"Beware of Lesbo limbo dancers!"

Appeals to the widespread interest in sporting events.

Yes, the Renaissance period in public washroom graffiti was a memorable one. The English and Art teachers of such talented creators must have been proud when they made the rounds of the facilities. However, to be fair, one can't ignore the possibility that the works were inscribed by those very same teachers.

In closing, a possible explanation for the current deterioration in graffiti was provided by a friend who speculates that the present crop of talented graffiti creators have relinquished public washrooms to amateurs and now hold forth on the Internet. If she is right, I may go electronic in my ensuite washroom so I can recreate the ambience of the past.

NEW BEGINNINGS

New day, new week, new month, new year,
new decade, new century, and new millennium.
In the rise and fall of empires, how will they unfold?

Will newly-anointed potentates continue rap-fiddling
while child/men warriors incinerate foliage and faceless
life, their pinkey-grey lung sacs shrivelling and cerebral
synapses short-circuiting from agent orange
and biologically 'smart' packaged insanities?

Will young Israeli soldiers, sweaty fingers on triggers,
maintain order among sacred relics of ancient faiths
of love and brotherhood, staring down intolerance
and constant flash points for bloody confrontations?

Will the sick and homeless still huddle over sidewalk
grates, wrapped in plastic sheets, through wintry holo-
causts
of public disregard, microcosms of all class distinctions
from life in the womb to the very old waiting to die?

Will children of the north and elsewhere choose
suicide over soul-destroying imprinted alien identities
or rediscover life in some self-fulfilling relationship
between the global village and ancestral bonds with
nature and spiritual trail markers?

Will mind-bending opiates of glitzy casinos,
provincial lotteries, staged brutality of sporting
extravaganzas, mayhem in media fare for all ages,
easy access to drugs, continue to divert us
from matters of national significance?

Will the quest for power in the guise of religions
continue to ignite holy wars, ethnic cleansing and
racial relocations, creating legions of maimed,
orphaned, neglected, abused and fearful remnants
of peaceful family units?

Will eco-systems in rainforest and old-stand northern
wilderness be clear-cut to feed appetites of urban
development and powerful multinationals working through
short-sighted governments, approving the pillaging
of natural resources, jobs and cultural identities?

Will space travel, space stations and Mars' habitations
devoid of nature be humankind's goals rather than . . . ?
        (to be continued)

Will discoveries in weapons of war, science, medicine,
and technology ever not be used?
        (to be continued)

Will the future driven by the Cyber-Techno Revolution
produce a less ignoble world?

Will headline news top 'Broccoli prevents prostrate
cancer'?

TIME AND SELF

(Dwell not unduly upon the future
for the present is all you have.)

The mo-ment
looms large

while past
frag-ments
and fu-ture
a-waits

but
all is il-lu-sion

for time
is a con-tin-u-um
with in-fin-i-ties
in both di-rec-tions

and self
a ma-te-ri-al-i-za-tion
of the in-stant

FIVE

HARDINESS

ILL WINDS

On a clear night, the lone yellow light from the dirty square window on the weathered plywood fish hut would have been visible from Cynwyd Castle, four miles away on Jackson's Point, Lake Simcoe. This night it was impossible in the heavy snow being hurled about by the roaring Arctic wind. Inside, it was as warm and as cozy as it ever gets in a fish hut.

In an unzipped, oil stained skidoo suit, the smaller of the two silent figures, a smouldering cigarette dangling from nicotine stained fingers, slouched back against the cold wall staring at the unmoving tip up whose monofilament line dropped vertically into the dark unknown. At the hole closest to the door, a hulk of a person in a scruffy, navy blue parka leaned forward, jigging the line up and down in the pristine eighty foot depths.

Harry rose stiffly, heel-butted his cigarette on the slushy floor and in a straddle position over the hole made an exaggerated version of a giraffe attempting a halftime stretch in an outhouse.

Laura, who outweighed her spouse by over a hundred pounds, raised her head and shook it disapprovingly, "Careful clown. If you fall in, don't expect me to go in after you."

Harry chuckled with a noticeable smoker's rasp as he envisaged his wife trying to dive into the hole to rescue him. "Cripes, I didn't know they made shoe horns that big."

"The only thing big around here is your mouth." With that, she bent forward and whipped a handful of water in his direction.

The smile on Harry's face diminished and for an instant, he considered reciprocating, but he knew from past experience that he nearly always came out of their playful competitions the loser.

"Shift back dear. I have to go out and water the petunias," said Harry as he sidestepped toward her.

"Oh you and your weak kidneys. If you didn't drink so much, you wouldn't be freezing the joint all the time. Come on. Make it snappy."

An observer of the exiting procedure in the cramped environs of the ice hut undoubtedly would have found it more hilarious than the giraffe routine.

It wasn't long before the door reopened and Harry stepped in. He didn't have to pull the door closed; the wind did it with a force which shook the small building.

"Brrr. Good to get the hell out of there. It's a storm and a half. Lot worse than before."

Then in his practiced Cagney voice, he said, "Well, you old fart, why don't you have a short snort." In his normal voice, he answered, "Thanks. Don't mind if I do. How about you, sweetheart?" He waved the mickey in her direction.

"You know what the doctor said about mixing pills and drinks. Strictly verboten," she answered, sounding annoyed.

"I still don't think a small nip would hurt. Probably improve your disposition." He laughed and after a considerable swallow turned his attention to the tip-up.

As if on cue, his line started to slowly rise and fall. Harry grabbed the wooden horizontal gently and felt the bated three hook spreader being move down below as something disturbed the live minnows. He sensed a sudden change in the shifting of the bait and pulled up sharply. The hook set, and Harry could feel the solid tugging of the unseen fish as it struggle frantically to rid itself of the thing in its mouth.

"It's a good one," Harry exclaimed as he hauled in the line hand-over-hand. The seconds seemed like minutes as the eighty feet of mono began to accumulate in large loops on the floor.

Laura felt excitement growing in her. No matter how

many times she went fishing, the magic of the moment never diminished.

As the head of the white fish broke the surface of the water, Harry yelled, "It's a dandy. Quick, the net."

It was over in an instant. The fish broke free and dropped into the waiting net. Laura could feel her heart beating fast and a slight tightness in her chest as the squirming seven pounder resisted Harry's efforts to remove it from the tangles of the mesh.

"It's not an award winner, but more than your basic keeper. Open the door, and I'll throw it out into the freezer."

Laura shifted slowly over to the exit and pivoting at the waist, put both hands on the rough planked door and pushed. It was like trying to move a brick wall, but it opened. The fish went flying out to the snow covered ice, and the door crashed shut again. The torrent of snow that entered, plastered the entrance and Laura.

Harry immediately noted that his wife said nothing as she brushed off her clothes. It wasn't like her. A fast quip about how he always got the best and warmest seat in the hut, etc., etc. would have been in order, but she said nothing.

"Are you OK, dear?"

"Yes, I'm fine. Just getting a little tired. Must be past my bedtime." She leaned back and commenced jigging, the line rubbing back and forth on the wooden edge of the floor opening. It wasn't the way.

Harry rebated his hooks and lowered them into the water, being careful to keep the coils on the floor from twisting or knotting as foot by foot the wet line slid over his fingers and into the depths. All the time, he sneaked sidelong glances in Laura's direction. He sensed something was up, but he knew better than to bug her if she were feeling tired or ill. He continued lowering his line until the slack told him that the bated spreader was in position, He set his tip up on the upright and adjusted the horizontal balance. He leaned back and lit up a cigarette from a crumpled package.

The next twenty minutes dragged by slowly for the duo without words as though both were concentrating on their fishing lines, and the sounds of the wind and hissing propane heater.

Finally, Laura set her fishing rod on the bench beside her. Reaching inside her parka, she retrieved a small plastic bottle and shook out a tiny white pill. Replacing the bottle in her inner pocket, she picked up the tablet carefully and placed it under her tongue. Then she leaned back, picked up the rod and reel, and commenced jigging as before.

Harry was aware of his wife's heart problems. Although the medications seemed to have her condition under control, both knew that at some future time, she would likely need some intrusive procedures. In the meantime, she was following the doctor's advice not to worry and get on with life.

Harry had misgivings about the ice fishing venture, especially overnight. There had been a brief argument, but in the end, she won. Laura's view of the good life always included an element of risk.

About ten minutes later and without any comment, Laura began to reel in her line with no effort to give the spoon any action. Part way up, the rod was almost jerked out of her hands, and the tip was pulled into the water in spite of her tightened grip. The line unwound from the reel with a hum as it angled off to the left of the hole. Gradually, she managed to gain control and turn the fish from its course away from the hut. As it turned, the line went slack, and she commenced to reel in as fast as possible. When she could feel resistance again, she turned to Harry and said, "Take over, will you?"

Astride the hole, Harry reeled in the fighting denizen, but his eyes were on his beloved.

She said softly, "Land him. You're dead meat if he gets away."

In the dim light of the hut lantern, it was impossible to be certain, but to Harry his wife's face had taken on a grey, putty-like tone. He reeled in as fast as he could. Almost as if the fish sensed the urgency of being landed, it ceased to struggle and was pulled quickly toward the light source of the hole in the ice. When it came into view, Harry, in one continuous coordinated motion, raised the rod, grabbed the nearby gaff hook, swung it into position and yanked the lake trout onto the floor. It was one of the fabled lunkers, well over thirty pounds, but it was of little interest to Harry.

He put his face close to Laura's and whispered, "Is it bad?" She nodded.

"I'm going out to start the truck. Will you be all right for a few moments?"

"Yes. Don't worry, the pills always take away the pain. But get your lazy ass moving," she said and smiled. But Harry knew that she was downplaying the seriousness of the situation.

The blast of cold air and snow which engulfed Laura when Harry exited seemed to help. She leaned back and tried to force her mind to control the pain coursing through her chest and arms. She was determined not to add to Harry's concern by screaming out.

It seemed like hours before the door was wrestled open, and a familiar snowman stepped into the doorway.

"Had trouble getting the old banger started. Had to use Spray Start in the carburetor. Are you hanging in OK?"

"Not bad, but hurry. Leave everything," she said and then to take the edge off her husband's anxiety, added, "Take the fish."

With strength born of necessity, the two staggered to the door of the truck and with much pushing and pulling managed to get the stricken woman inside. Then, Harry retrieved the now frozen white fish and the still quivering lake trout and tossed them into the back of the pickup.

Harry checked to ensure the four wheel drive was engaged before shifting into drive. The truck moved ahead slowly, the knobby tires clawing into the drifting snow. Windshield wipers clicked back and forth against the lashing snow. However, even with the yellow fog lights on, visibility was as close to zero as white-out conditions produce.

Anyone who fishes Lake Simcoe in winter will acknowledge their gratitude to the commercial fish hut operators who set route markers of evergreens upright in the ice every three to five hundred feet from shore to offshore clusters of huts.

In his mind's eye, Harry knew approximately where the closest evergreen was in relation to their hut. He drove slowly into the white wall of swirling snow. Visibility varied from zero to three to four feet. He broke the silence with an excited, "There!" pointing ahead and slightly to the left. The truck barely missed the tree bending animatedly in the wind.

"That's good, Harry. Just find the next and the next and we'll soon be out of here." Her voice was barely audible over the roar of the wind and the growl of the old engine.

Harry turned off the dashboard lights to enhance the limited effectiveness of the headlights. As a consequence, he had to rely on his wife's movements and speech to inform him of her state of consciousness.

The thin man gripped the steering wheel hard as he hunched forward scanning intensely for the next marker. The lake was crisscrossed by patchwork tracks of cars, Bombardiers, Skidoos, ATV's (All Terrain Vehicles) and innumerable trucks. There was no guarantee that the trail he seemed to be following was the road to shore.

Suddenly the dark shape of a marker passed several feet to the left. Harry smiled. If their luck held out, they would be on shore in less than ten minutes. If he headed directly to the ambulance unit in Sutton, they would have her in Emergency in the York County Hospital in Newmarket in about forty-five minutes. Although the paramedics didn't have the sophisticated ambulance-to-hospital radio hookups of Toronto, they did have the training, basic equipment and drugs to deal with heart arrest and other symptoms of cardiac problems.

Less than two minutes transpired before Harry was certain he had strayed from the ice road. After the first two markers, there had been none. He was lost. It was impossible to keep the vehicle going in a straight line. Each time he hit a snow drift, the truck would veer one way or the other and his efforts to steer back on course sometimes caused the vehicle to spin in a circle. He cursed his lack of foresight in not having brought a compass.

Laura hadn't moved for some minutes, and Harry's yells to her hadn't brought any response. He didn't dare stop. Time was the enemy, and his only strategy was to get off the ice as quickly as possible. Blindly he pressed forward, adjusting his direction by instinct.

About three minutes later, the old GMC crashed into a pressure ridge. The truck ran up the slope of broken ice sheets and tilted downward to a bone rattling stop. Although the front wheels were in the water, the frame of the pickup appeared to be caught solidly on the edge of the jagged ice. The engine was still running.

The jolt brought Laura to consciousness and she exclaimed, "What the hell was that?"

"It's the pressure ridge to the west of Georgina Island. There isn't another like it in the area. The mainland is off to the right," he answered. "I'm going for help. I'll leave the motor running, and you should be warm enough 'till I get back. Has the pain gone down some?"

In the beam of the flashlight he could see her nod. "OK, I won't be long," he said.

Harry pushed open the door and pulled himself along the side of the truck to the back and then slid down the west side of the ridge to the flat ice. He struck out in a southeasterly direction with the wind pushing at his back and frigid drafts finding their way under his upturned collar and pulled down touque.

* * *

Laura had been drifting in and out of consciousness for some time. Although the pain had lost its sharp edges, she knew the problem hadn't gone away. She'd taken more nitro tablets than any doctor had ever sanctioned, but she knew that the drug was keeping her alive. In the reverie of semi- consciousness her mind had begun roving over her past life with Harry when suddenly she was brought to alertness by a slight movement of the vehicle.

She pushed down on the door handle. The lock released and the door opened to admit a blast of cold air and snow. It felt good.

At that moment, the GMC lurched forward, and slowly crunched further down into the open water of the fissure. Laura pushed the door wide, and it immediately jammed against the jumbled ice. Realizing that the truck might plunge into the freezing water, she pivoted to place her feet on the rough ice of the slope and pulled herself out of the sinking vehicle. There were sufficient rough edges to the piled ice to allow her to gain footholds and move back to the safety of the flat frozen lake.

Although the constriction in her chest had not gone away, the buffeting of the frigid air seemed to ease the critical internal problem. She knew that she couldn't make it to shore. Her only hope was to stay alive until help arrived.

* * *

Harry plodded step by step through the deepening drifts, hoping to keep in a straight line. Veering to either side could result in his walking along or away from shore. He tried to keep the unreliable wind at his back as he moved forward like an automaton lunging into the blinding snow. Suddenly, the shin of his right leg banged against a raised obstacle, and he fell face down onto the rough planks of a small dock.

He had made it to shore. But where? He pushed to his feet. There would have to be a building or cottage nearby. Then he saw it, the hulking outline of a stained wood-sided building. It was in darkness.

The exhausted man stumbled along side the house to the road. Out of the gloom appeared a street light in a halo of yellow. He turned right. The road was already drifting in and would soon be impassable to traffic if in fact there were any permanent residents on it.

Harry's strength was ebbing fast. His face and wrists were beyond pain. Miniature ice sculptures covered his eyebrows and moustache and snow was packed around the folds of his skidoo suit. If he fell, he knew that he might not get up.

He had passed a number of street lights and darkened houses when he saw lights coming toward him. Soon he could discern the flashing blue lights of a township plow. He stood in the centre of the road and waved his arms slowly.

The plow was moving at a reduced speed because of the poor visibility, and when the driver spotted the snow covered figure, he brought the large truck to a stop within feet of a collision. The person bathed in the headlights of the plow didn't move, and the driver got out to determine the problem.

When Harry was safely in the warm cab, he explained the crisis in a voice strained with fatigue and distress. The driver was immediately on the radio to his dispatcher. Emergency forces were summoned, and in less than fifteen minutes, the police rescue unit complete with amphibian ice/watercraft on a trailer was parked behind the plow.

When Harry described the location, the officers knew exactly where the pressure ridge was and in a flurry of efficiency, had the rescue unit off the trailer and warming up, its huge propeller swirling snow with a powerful whine.

Harry insisted on joining the policemen in the rescue attempt and eased inside to the back bench of the small cabin. The air boat was soon moving across the frozen surface, skimming over snow drifts and wind blown ice. Within minutes, the powerful headlights and sweeping searchlight picked up the pressure ridge, and the driver turned the craft to follow it in a northwesterly direction. As they slid over the ice surface, Harry peered anxiously out the frosted side window which he kept cleared with his mitts.

Although it seemed like forever, it wasn't more than ten minutes when the officer in the passenger's seat shouted over the roar of the engine, "There! I see something."

The deafening sound of the engine eased as the accelerator was released. The spotlight picked out the dim outline of the rear of the pickup truck. It was almost vertical in the air. The cab had slipped nearly out of sight into the waters and only the rear wheels and frame were caught, preventing it from submerging entirely.

"My God," moaned Harry. "I left her in the cab. There's no way she could have survived." He lowered his head into his hands.

The police got out and climbed the sloping ice ridge to direct a flashlight into the interior of what remained of the cab above water.

"The right side door is open and I don't see anyone

inside," yelled one of the men over the howling wind.

They returned to the amphibian and the driver said, "Your wife isn't inside. She must have got out before the cab went under. She can't have gone far. We'll spread out and search along the ice ridge to the southeast. We'll go three abreast, four feet apart."

Harry took the position closest to the jumbled ice and for most of the time was part way up the slope. They moved slowly kicking snow piles and anything which might be other than a natural formation.

About twenty feet past the partially submerged GMC, Harry kicked at a sizable drift and was rewarded by the feel of something softer than ice and more substantial than snow. He dropped to his knees and with both hands, began scooping away the drifted snow. The shape of a parka hood came into view. The police joined him, and the body of the stricken woman was quickly uncovered.

The two officers put their hands under her arms and hoisted the body erect. Harry brushed away snow caked on his wife's face. His words were unintelligible to the officers in the noisy wind. The men leaned the torso back, and Harry picked up the feet. It was a struggle, but the trio managed to carry Laura back to the ice craft and get her inside.

In the overhead light of the cabin, they were able to see the face clearly. Suddenly, the ice incrusted lids quivered and opened.

Harry exclaimed, "She's alive. Thank God."

He removed his gloves and place his hands on the blue grey cheeks of his beloved. They had the feel of deep frozen ice. As the warmth of his body flowed into hers, her lips parted, she smiled and then, as if she knew that the situation was under control, eye lids slowly closed over tired blue eyes.

While Harry was concentrating on his wife, the driver turned the amphibian around and headed quickly toward shore in a direction that he knew would take them directly to the marina at Jackson's Point. The other officer radioed headquarters, arranging for an ambulance and medical help to be there when they arrived.

* * *

Several weeks later in York County Hospital, where Laura was recovering from the angioplasty procedure and the amputation of three toes on her right foot, she reviewed her ordeal with her husband.

"When I was on the ice and could feel the hands of death on me, I entered a place which I know was the passageway to Heaven. The chilling cold disappeared, and I could feel the warmth of brilliant lights of the new place to which I was going. Ahead I could see family and loved ones who had gone before, waiting with arms outstretched to welcome me. It was then that I thought I could hear your voice telling me not to go. I knew I couldn't leave you. I had to go back. The cold returned when I felt the jolt of your boot kicking at my waist."

"Well, my love, you made the right decision. But I'm not sure whether it was me that brought you back or the three fish that I retrieved from the back of the old truck. . . . You can bet that as soon as you get home, we're gonna have the best damn fish fry we ever had."